GEARING UP FOR SPORTS!

BASKETBALL GEAR

NOAH RICCARDI

PowerKiDS press.

Published in 2027 by The Rosen Publishing Group, Inc.
2544 Clinton Street, Buffalo, NY 14224

First Edition

Book Design: Madison Thogmartin

Photo Credits: Cover, p. 1 wavebreakmedia/Shutterstock.com; p. 5 Brocreative/Shutterstock.com; p. 7 P. J. McDonnell/Shutterstock.com; p. 9 Pukhov K./Shutterstock.com; p. 11 Mark Fann/Shutterstock.com; p. 13 A. Ricardo/Shutterstock.com; p. 15 Oleksandr Osipov/Shutterstock.com; p. 17 Igor Panevski/Shutterstock.com; p. 19 artyaroslav/Shutterstock.com; p. 21 photoyh/Shutterstock.com.

Cataloging-in-Publication Data
Names: Riccardi, Noah.
Title: Basketball gear / Noah Riccardi.
Description: Buffalo, New York : PowerKids Press, 2027. | Series: Gearing up for sports! | Includes glossary and index.
Identifiers: ISBN 9781499456646 (pbk.) | ISBN 9781499456653 (library bound) | ISBN 9781499456660 (ebook)
Subjects: LCSH: Basketball--Juvenile literature. | Basketball--Equipment and supplies--Juvenile literature.
Classification: LCC GV885.1 R533 2027 | DDC 796.323--dc23

Manufactured in China

CPSIA Compliance Information: Batch #QS27PK. For Further Information contact Rosen Publishing, at 1-800-237-9932.

CONTENTS

The Basketball

Basketball players try to throw a ball into a net. This ball is called a basketball. The ball's outside is made from **leather**. It has small bumps and is easy to grip. The basketball is **inflated** with air.

Basketballs come in different sizes. Pro leagues use full-size balls. Young players use smaller balls. This lets people of all hand sizes play basketball. A full-size ball would be too big for young players.

Wilson
NCAA
OFFICIAL GAME BALL
7 | 29.5"
NCAA® EVO NXT GAME BALL
EVOLUTION
EVOLUTION GAME BALL
SIZE 6
NCAA
RHYTHM
NCAA® RHYTHM
NBA TAKEOFF

Jerseys

Teams wear jerseys in different colors. This helps players know who to pass to. Jerseys also have numbers. This helps people tell players apart. Some jerseys also have player names on the back.

4

Basketball jerseys are usually shirts without sleeves. They are made from light **fabrics**. This helps players stay cool while playing. During the game, players must tuck their jerseys into their shorts.

SMU
0

Mouthguards

Players might get hit by the ball. Other players might run into them. Mouthguards protect a player's teeth and mouth when this happens. Mouthguards are made of plastic. They may be **molded** to a player's teeth for a good fit.

USA
4

Referee's Whistle

The **referees** of a basketball game each have whistles. The whistle is loud so all players and fans can hear it. A referee blows the whistle to stop play after a foul or if the ball goes out of bounds.

FIBA

Shoes

Basketball players wear special shoes when on the **court**. The **soles** of basketball shoes are bouncy so players can jump higher. The shoes may also have high tops to keep players' ankles **stable**.

ITALIA
SPALDING
HUNGARY
9

Basketball shoes can have special designs. Players wear these shoes to express themselves. Michael Jordan was a famous basketball star. He helped design his own shoes. Fans could buy them, too. Jordan shoes became **fashion** items off the court.

AIR JORDAN

Headbands

Players with long hair often wear headbands. This keeps hair out of their eyes. Players also use headbands for fashion. Allen Iverson was a star player in the 2000s. Iverson was known for wearing headbands.

4
hummel

GLOSSARY

court: The place where a basketball game is played.

fabrics: Types of cloth.

fashion: A style of clothing that is popular at a certain time.

inflated: Filled with air or other gas.

leather: A material made from an animal's skin.

molded: Shaped to fit.

referees: People who make sure players follow the rules of the game.

soles: The bottoms of shoes.

stable: Firm and steady.

FOR MORE INFORMATION

BOOKS

Abdo, Kenny. *Basketball GOATs*. Minneapolis, MN: Abdo Publishing, 2025.

Wagner, Zelda. *Basketball Superstars*. Minneapolis, MN: Lerner Publications, 2025.

WEBSITES

Olympics: Basketball
olympics.com/en/sports/basketball/
Learn about basketball at the Olympic Games.

Sports Engine Play: Basketball Terms Explained
discover.sportsengineplay.com/basketball/basketball-terms-explained/
Learn some of the words people use to talk about basketball.

INDEX